Table of Contents

Beating the System: Exposing the Truth and Fighting Back Against a Rigged Federal Justice System

The federal game is rigged, and the house always wins. But this isn't a game—it's the harsh reality of a federal justice system weaponized by the government to maintain control and suppress dissent. Federal prosecutors, acting as henchmen for the regime, relentlessly chase convictions with no regard for real justice. Agents of the FBI and other federal law enforcement, emboldened by badges of authority, routinely twist laws to feed the oppressive federal machine. Overburdened federal public defenders are set up to fail by an inherently unequal system stacked against the defendant's interests

ARDIT FERIZI

For corporate deals, bulk purchases, or any other inquiries about my book, "Beating the System: Exposing the Truth and Fighting Back Against a Rigged Federal Justice System" please contact me at ardit.ferizi@protonmail.com. Thank you for your interest and support.

COPYRIGHT © 2024 BY Ardit Ferizi

The author and publisher have made every effort to ensure the accuracy of the information herein. However, the information contained in this book is sold without warranty, either express or implied.

Disclaimer: This book, including all insights, strategies, and opinions presented herein, is intended for informational and educational purposes only. The author and publisher are not offering it as legal advice, nor should it be considered a substitute for legal advice from a qualified attorney. Laws and legal procedures are subject to frequent changes and can vary widely in different jurisdictions. Readers are advised to consult with a qualified legal professional before making any legal decisions. The author and publisher disclaim any liability, loss, or risk, personal or otherwise, which is incurred as a consequence, directly or indirectly, of the use and application of any of the contents of this book.

Understanding the Federal Criminal Procedure: A Brutal Odyssey Through a Rigged System

The journey through the federal criminal justice system is a merciless gauntlet, expertly designed by a system rigged against the defendant from the start. This serves as a grim roadmap through the procedural abyss, exposing the harsh reality for those entangled in the system, from their initial capture to the suffocating grip of post-conviction.

Investigation: The onset of oppression, where federal agencies deploy an arsenal of surveillance, wiretaps, and warrants—not in the name of justice, but as mechanisms of control, marking the unsuspecting individual for the system's cruel game.

Arrest: The chilling moment the system's jaws clamp shut, typically through a warrant issued under a guise of probable cause, violently uprooting the individual from their life into the nightmarish reality of federal accusation.

Booking: At a Federal Detention Center or a contracted facility—a purgatory where federal detainees are mixed with state inmates—the suspect undergoes a process that strips them of their identity, reducing them to mere digits in the federal behemoth's ledger.

Initial Appearance: The defendant's coerced debut in court, where charges are starkly outlined, and the facade of rights and bail is presented, underscoring a stark power imbalance designed to intimidate and subdue.

Detention Hearing: A harrowing stage to determine if the defendant is to be granted a semblance of freedom or further entombed within the system's clutches, highlighting the skewed notion of risk versus control.

Grand Jury/Indictment: A facade of justice where a grand jury, swayed by prosecutorial manipulation, decides if the concocted evidence suffices to chain the defendant formally to the wheels of the federal prosecutorial machine.

Arraignment: The stage for the formal imposition of charges, compelling the defendant to plead within the court's oppressive theatre, a vivid reminder of the crushing machinery of justice arrayed against them.

Discovery: A phase masquerading as evidence exchange, where the prosecution grudgingly parcels out information, wielding delay and obfuscation as weapons to maintain their stranglehold over the narrative.

Pre-Trial Motions: Battles of legal wits, where attempts to challenge the prosecution's overreach are often smothered by a judiciary complicit in maintaining the system's unyielding facade of righteousness.

Plea Bargaining: The dark art of judicial coercion, where defendants are cornered into sacrificing their pursuit of justice on the altar of expediency, a grotesque perversion of the notion of choice.

Trial: The ultimate spectacle, purporting to be the arena of justice but often unfolding as a predetermined tragedy, where the scales are irrevocably tipped against the defendant.

Verdict: The culmination of the ordeal, often a mere formality endorsing the prosecution's narrative, sealing the defendant's fate with the cold finality of institutional endorsement.

Sentencing: A phase that dispenses not justice but vengeance, indifferent to the nuances of the individual's circumstances, a testament to the system's insatiable appetite for punishment over rehabilitation.

Appeals: A daunting path strewn with obstacles, where attempts to challenge the unjust outcomes are met with a system protective of its own, a bulwark against the aspirations of those it has wronged.

Post-Conviction: The aftermath, where the convict navigates the ruins of their life under the long shadow of their ordeal, forever branded by a system that discards them on the periphery of society.

The Unwritten Rules of Prison Life: Navigating the Inmate Code

In the stark, unforgiving environment of prison, survival hinges not just on adhering to the official regulations set forth by the institution, but also on navigating an intricate web of unwritten rules established by the convict population itself. This inmate code, a complex blend of ethics, survival tactics, and social norms, serves as an essential guide for those seeking to endure their sentence with the least amount of trouble. Understanding and respecting these rules can mean the difference between maintaining a semblance of peace and facing relentless hardships.

Silence is Golden: Above all, do not betray others. Informing on anyone while in prison will not help you in any way; it will only label you as a snitch, a cardinal sin that can lead to dire consequences. Even staff themselves dislike filling out paperwork, so instead, they may punish you with excessive solitary confinement, transfer you, label you a 'security threat,' and generally regard you as a 'hot potato'—universally disliked and bound to suffer greatly. The code of silence is paramount.

Racial Lines: The prison population is often divided along racial lines, a divisive legacy that can dictate social interactions. Fraternizing with convicts of another race may endanger your safety. Recognize and respect these boundaries for your well-being.

Autonomy: Keep to yourself and exercise vigilance. Your affairs are yours alone; entanglement in others' matters can only lead to trouble. Apply your common sense liberally and without fail.

Chow Hall Politics: Meal times are governed by an unspoken racial/gang segregation. Observe and adhere to these seating arrangements to avoid conflict.

Hygiene is Mandatory: Personal cleanliness is not optional. Regular showers are expected, and washing hands after using the bathroom is a must. Neglecting hygiene can provoke hostility from fellow convicts.

Respect the Elders: Longevity in prison earns respect. Older convicts have survived through wisdom and strength. Acknowledge their status and learn from their experience.

Stand Your Ground: When challenged, you must be willing to defend yourself physically. Attempting to avoid confrontation through negotiation is perceived as weakness. It's better to fight and lose than not to fight at all.

Avoid Debts: Do not gamble or borrow, especially with promises of future repayment. Incurring debt without the means for prompt repayment invites trouble.

Protective Custody Perils: Requesting protective custody can mark you for the remainder of your sentence, making you a target. Once labeled as needing protection, the stigma follows you everywhere.

Language Matters: Within these walls, you are a convict, not an inmate. The latter term is seen as derogatory, suggesting weakness or unreliability. Language is a powerful tool for either integration or alienation.

Additionally, the core principles of "Don't snitch, Don't get in debt, Don't let no one mess with you," serve as the bedrock of prison conduct. Adhering to these principles can safeguard one's physical and mental integrity within the correctional facility.

Navigating prison life according to these unwritten codes demands a delicate balance of strength, wisdom, and discretion. These rules, born from the collective experience of countless individuals who have traversed the harsh reality of prison life, provide a framework for maintaining one's dignity and safety in an environment that often seeks to strip away both.

Table of Contents

Part 1: The Federal Court Gauntlet

Part 2: The Snitch System and Self-Sabotage

Part 3: Surviving and Thriving Post-Sentencing

Part 4: The Broader Battle

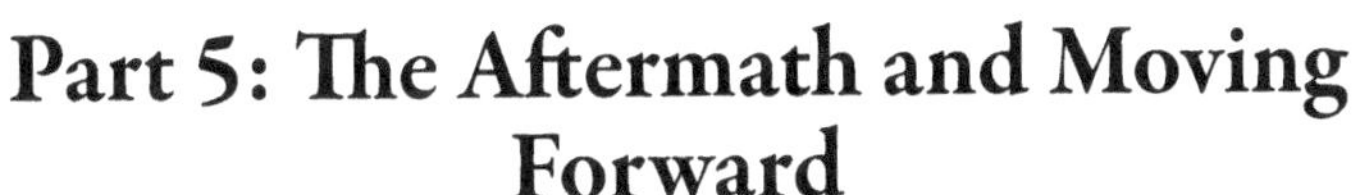

Part 5: The Aftermath and Moving Forward

Introduction

"**B**eating the System: Exposing the Truth and Fighting Back Against a Rigged Federal Justice System" is not just a title; it's a manifesto, a battle plan against a justice system manipulated to oppress rather than uphold. In the heart of this struggle stands Ardit Ferizi, whose harrowing journey through the U.S. Department of Justice unveils the grim reality of a system weaponized by the government. This narrative exposes a federal justice system where fairness is a myth, and the scales of justice are skewed to serve the interests of those in power, systematically targeting dissent and suppressing freedom under the guise of law and order.

Ardit Ferizi's tale is one of resilience against an overwhelming adversary. From his initial chilling experiences in the confines of Sungai Buloh prison to the entanglement in the U.S. Federal justice system without ever setting foot in the United States, his story sheds light on the systemic injustices and the corrupt tactics employed by federal prosecutors and law enforcement agencies. These entities, driven by a perverse incentive to secure convictions at any cost, engage in practices that trample upon civil liberties and exploit the vulnerable, leaving a trail of ruined lives in their wake.

"Beating the System" goes beyond recounting Ferizi's personal saga; it serves as an essential guide for navigating the treacherous waters of the federal justice process. It meticulously deconstructs the federal court gauntlet, from the manipulation of evidence to the coercion of guilty pleas through the sinister roles of jailhouse informants and the deceptive allure of proffer sessions. This book equips its readers with the knowledge to recognize and combat the oppressive strategies of the federal justice system, advocating for a reformation that ensures justice serves the people, not the prosecutorial agenda.

Through the lens of Ardit Ferizi's confrontation with a system more invested in convictions than justice, "Beating the System" illuminates the dark corners of federal justice, revealing the tyrannical figures who, under the cloak of honor, perpetrate systemic injustices. It is a clarion call for action, urging readers to stand against the rigged game played in the shadowy corridors of federal power. This journey through the labyrinth of the federal justice system is not only Ardit's; it's a rallying cry for all who dream of a just world, making "Beating the System" a beacon of hope for those ensnared by a flawed system and a guide for dismantling the machinery of oppression. Welcome to the heart of darkness within the federal justice system, illuminated by the unwavering light of truth and the relentless pursuit of justice.

Ardit Ferizi

Beating the System: Exposing the Truth and Fighting Back Against a Rigged Federal Justice System

ARDIT FERIZI

1. Entering the Arena: The Initial Appearance and Bail Battles

From the moment you step into the cold, soulless federal courthouse for your initial appearance, a suffocating air of dread envelopes you, signaling your entrance not into a place of justice and fairness, but into a veritable gladiator's pit. Here, the scales of justice are not just tipped but wholly upended, calibrated for your downfall in a system that relishes your despair. You are not a participant in a judicial process; you are prey in a hunt, where federal prosecutors, the bloodthirsty hounds of a corrupt regime, salivate at the prospect of your demise.

This inaugural plunge into the abyss of the federal justice system is a meticulously orchestrated farce, a charade where the concept of bail is twisted into a grotesque tool of class warfare and subjugation. The halls of justice morph into a grotesque marketplace, where your freedom, dignity, and future are auctioned off to the highest bidder under the guise of legal procedure. The government, cloaked in a veneer of legitimacy, reveals itself as the executioner, eagerly awaiting the chance to feed another soul to the insatiable beast of its prison industrial complex.

In this arena, federal prosecutors emerge as the emperors of cruelty, their so-called victories a testament not to justice served but to lives destroyed in the name of ambition and the federal justice machine's ravenous appetite. The system, powered by an endless reservoir of resources and a fanatical commitment to crush dissent, casts a looming shadow over any notion of freedom or fairness, thriving on fear and the maintenance of a status quo that serves only the interests of the powerful.

Amidst this bleak landscape, however, a flicker of defiance burns within the hearts of the accused. To stand before the federal government's juggernaut is to face a stark ultimatum: bow to a system that has long forsaken any pretense of justice or stand tall against the tyranny of a regime that wields law and order as weapons of oppression. The path forward is fraught with danger, yet it is also lined with the promise of resistance. Within the crucible of the federal courthouse, the true struggle unfolds—a battle not merely for exoneration but for the very essence of justice itself.

The federal justice system, with its blatant preference for punishment over fairness and its disdainful disregard for the individual, stands as a mockery of the principles it purports to uphold. As you navigate these treacherous waters, bear in mind that the battle ahead is not solely for your own liberation but for the dismantling of a despotic machine that masquerades as a bastion of justice. In this war, knowledge is your arsenal, resilience your armor, and truth the beacon that guides your way.

2. The Grand Illusion: Navigating The Grand Jury's Veil of Secrecy

In the darkest underbelly of the federal justice system lurks the grand jury, a tool of manipulation so perverse, it mocks the very notion of justice it purports to serve. This chapter tears away the facade of the grand illusion, exposing a theater of secrecy and deceit where the fates of the accused are mercilessly sealed, far removed from the light of day and the eyes of public accountability. Here, in these shadowed assemblies of injustice, the government, with its iron fist, conducts its orchestration of outcomes that bear no resemblance to transparency or fairness.

Transformed from a supposed shield against unfounded charges into a vile weapon of prosecutorial overreach, the grand jury has become nothing more than a grotesque puppet, its strings pulled by the whims of federal prosecutors. Encased in a shroud of secrecy, these prosecutors wield their unchecked power, presenting one-sided tales of guilt without the hindrance of a defense or the discerning eye of a judge. In this Kafkaesque nightmare, the voices of the accused are smothered, their stories untold, and the possibility of defense obliterated.

What was once heralded as a cornerstone of citizen protection has been twisted into a monstrous tool of indictment, used with reckless abandon. The adage "a grand jury would indict a ham sandwich" has evolved from a dark joke into a tragic commentary on a system derailed, a place where the bar for accusing someone of a crime is abysmally low, obliterating the presumption of innocence.

This grand illusion is a critical battlefield, not a mere formality, where the scales of justice are not just tipped but wholly cast aside in favor of the prosecution. The veil of secrecy enveloping these proceedings is not for the protection of integrity but a cloak for the sinister maneuvers of a prosecution hell-bent on indictments at any price. Here, behind the closed doors of this judicial farce, a narrative is spun from the selective presentation of evidence, often unchecked for truth, transforming the grand jury from an independent evaluator to a mere echo chamber for government propaganda.

The grand jury system has been effectively castrated, reduced to a rubber-stamping apparatus that propels the prosecutorial agenda forward, trampling over the ruins of fairness and due process. Fighting against this clandestine charade is like battling phantoms; the accused and their defenders grope in the dark, seeking justice in a system designed to disorient and subdue.

The existence of the grand jury as it stands today is a testament to the federal government's chilling expertise in legal deception and procedural tyranny. It symbolizes not merely a failure of justice but a calculated attack on the very bedrock of democratic principles. For those ensnared by its web, the grand jury process is a plunge into an abyss, a system where verdicts are preordained and the rights of the accused are an afterthought, discarded on the altar of expedience.

Challenging this grand illusion demands unwavering vigilance and courage to peel away the layers of deceit and confront the colossus of federal injustice head-on. It is an imperative struggle, not only for the vindication of individual rights but for the soul of a justice system that has veered disastrously from its foundational ideals. The grand jury, in its monstrous form, stands as a grim monument to these failures, a beacon of injustice that must be dismantled and rebuilt if there is ever to be a glimmer of true justice.

3. Arraignment and Pleas: The First Taste of Federal Injustice

The ordeal known as the federal justice system doesn't begin with a semblance of fairness but with a grotesque farce called arraignment, where the mirage of justice is ruthlessly dismantled. Enclosed within the stifling walls of a courtroom—ostensibly a sanctuary of justice—the arraignment degenerates into an outright ambush, a carefully staged atrocity where defendants are methodically divested of their dignity and their right to be presumed innocent until proven guilty.

As a litany of charges echoes through the chamber, the arraignment discloses its malignant core—not a simple step in procedural formality but the opening volley in a psychological onslaught orchestrated by the state. The federal system, grotesquely armed with an arsenal of inflated charges and severe sentencing threats, launches its attack, marking the defendant not as a person presumed innocent but as prey targeted by the inexorable gears of government oppression. The atmosphere thickens with coercion, presenting the accused with a harrowing choice: to utter a coerced plea of guilt, shadowed by the specter of draconian sentences, or to brave the Kafkaesque nightmare of a trial, hopelessly skewed against them from the outset.

Here, the depraved incentives driving the federal justice behemoth are starkly exposed—a monstrosity not designed for the noble quest for truth or justice but engineered for the sinister, calculated extraction of guilty pleas. The plea bargaining process, masquerading as a paragon of judicial efficiency, is revealed for what it truly is: a mechanism of extortion. Defendants find themselves ensnared, forced into a dire decision: submit beneath the crushing weight of the government's demands or confront the despotism of a trial, with scales so grievously tilted that justice becomes a grotesque parody.

This reliance on plea bargains unmasks the federal government's essence—not as a guardian of justice but as a tyrant deploying its might to extort compliance. This corruption of the adversarial legal system not only ridicules the foundational belief that truth emerges from the confrontation of opposing arguments but also annihilates the constitutional protections meant to shield individuals from the overreach of a tyrannical state. The plea deal, in this dystopian reality, morphs not into a mutually agreed compromise but a diktat from the throne of autocracy, where the state's so-called leniency is nothing more than a mirage, conditional upon the defendant's total capitulation.

As the drama of this charade unfolds, the arraignment and plea stages reveal themselves not as the initiation of a legal process but as the first steps into a panopticon designed for oppression. The government, ravenous for convictions, wields the machinery of "justice" with unrestrained malice, transforming human lives into expendable elements in a rigged game with a foregone conclusion. In this context, the act of pleading not guilty becomes a critical maneuver for the accused, a strategic play to access discovery materials essential for mounting a defense, potentially leading to motions to suppress evidence or even to dismiss the case entirely—a glimmer of agency in navigating the treacherous labyrinth of a system so deeply marred by corruption that to name it "justice" is an exercise in Orwellian doublespeak.

Navigating the poisonous currents of arraignment and plea bargaining demands more than mere resilience; it requires a relentless resolve to resist the tyranny ingrained in these preliminary stages of the federal inquisition. This battle for justice transcends the plight of the individual, challenging the core of a system that has deviated so drastically from its professed ideals of fairness and equity as to be rendered unrecognizable. Armed with the shield of knowledge and the sword of defiance, defendants and their allies are called to storm the battlements, determined to dismantle the fortress of coercion that epitomizes the federal justice system, and in its ruins, demand a restoration of justice and human dignity in its purest form.

4. Discovery Wars: Unmasking Prosecutorial Hide-and-Seek

Within the shadowy depths of the federal justice system, the discovery phase degenerates into a perverse theater of war, where the ideals of transparency and fairness are not just ignored but actively desecrated. This stage, dubbed the Discovery Wars, reveals a dystopian battlefield where defendants are ensnared in a Kafkaesque game of hide-and-seek, pitted against a government that wields its colossal investigative powers not for the pursuit of justice, but as instruments of oppression.

Armed with a staggering array of surveillance and evidence-gathering behemoths, the federal behemoth mocks its duty to disclose evidence, indulging instead in a culture of deceit and procrastination. Prosecutors, ostensibly bound by duty to reveal exculpatory evidence, engage in a duplicitous game of strategic withholding, doling out scraps of information with calculated miserliness to cripple the defense's preparations.

This malignant strategy doesn't merely hinder the accused's ability to mount an effective defense; it is an affront to the very essence of justice, corroding the principle that justice must be pursued in the light, not cloaked in shadows.

The so-called discovery phase thus metamorphoses into a gauntlet of prosecutorial gatekeeping, where vital evidence capable of dismantling the government's concocted narratives or highlighting investigative malfeasance remains entombed in a quagmire of obfuscation. The defense is relegated to a Sisyphean task, forced to cobble together a coherent defense from the meager tidbits grudgingly conceded by a prosecution hell-bent on safeguarding its dominion.

This grotesque manipulation of the discovery process is a stark aberration from the vision of a balanced legal system, unveiling a realm where the obsession with securing convictions eclipses any semblance of a quest for justice. Here, the government, in its fanatical pursuit of victory, blinds itself to its cardinal obligation to truth and fairness. Defendants, ostensibly shielded by the presumption of innocence, are instead compelled to defend themselves shackled, stripped of the critical arsenal of evidence necessary for their vindication.

As the Discovery Wars escalate, the defense's

mission transcends the mere unearthing of concealed evidence. It becomes a crusade to unearth and dismantle the systemic injustices that fertilize the ground for such prosecutorial malpractice to flourish. This struggle is not merely for the salvation of individual defendants but a battle for the soul of a justice system that has deviated so far from its foundational tenets of fairness and transparency as to become unrecognizable.

Navigating this malevolent labyrinth demands a vigilance, tenacity, and an unyielding dedication to the ideals of justice that are antithetical to the current state of affairs. It necessitates a radical overhaul of the discovery rules and a relentless drive to hold the prosecution accountable for its dereliction of duty. As this narrative of confrontation unfolds, the saga of the discovery phase becomes a pivotal chapter in the larger narrative of resistance and reform—a clarion call to action against a judicial apparatus that has perverted the noble pursuit of justice into a dark carnival of victory at any cost.

5. Motions in Limine: Cutting the Gag Before It Silences You

In the corrupted heart of federal litigation lies a battleground steeped in deceit and manipulation, where motions in limine stand as the besieged defendant's last bastion against a prosecutorial onslaught that knows no bounds of fairness or integrity. These pre-trial skirmishes, far from mere procedural formalities, are the defendant's desperate counterstrike in a rigged game, an attempt to fend off the government's relentless efforts to corrupt the scales of justice with evidence tainted by prejudice, irrelevance, or outright illegality.

The federal government, drunk on its own power and armed with a dubious arsenal of so-called evidence, launches its attack with the zeal of an oppressor. Its objective is clear: to inundate the courtroom with material designed not to illuminate truth but to cloud judgment, to prejudice the jury, and to contaminate the court's view of the defendant. Within this treacherous terrain of legal warfare and judicial discretion, the defense wages a guerrilla campaign, challenging the inclusion of evidence that fails to meet the legal system's purported standards of relevance, reliability, and fairness.

Motions in limine thus transform from procedural steps to critical weapons in the defense's arsenal, wielded in a frantic effort to ensure that the trial remains a contest based on facts rather than a grotesque spectacle of the government's capacity to defame, to insinuate guilt by mere association, and to leverage evidence procured by dubious means—be it through the breach of constitutional sanctities, the abuse of surveillance technologies, or reliance on the testimonies of witnesses whose credibility is as substantial as a house of cards.

The war over these motions shines a merciless light on the broader conflict against a justice system that has shamelessly abandoned the principles of due process and the rights of the accused on the altar of expediency, national security, and prosecutorial aggrandizement. By contesting the admissibility of evidence, the defense does more than protect the sanctity of the trial; it exposes the sordid depths to which the government will sink in its unholy crusade for convictions at any cost.

This critical juncture in the legal process becomes not just a moment of legal maneuvering but a stark revelation of the defense's monumental task: to wrest control of the narrative from the clutches of a government hell-bent on securing a guilty verdict by any means necessary. It is an uphill battle to ensure that the evidence is weighed on its merits, untainted by the poison of governmental overreach and prosecutorial misconduct—a fight to reclaim the very soul of justice from the jaws of a system that has mutated into a monstrosity of injustice.

As the defense navigates the minefield of motions in limine, the wider implications of this struggle come sharply into focus. It encapsulates the dire struggle for justice within a system grotesquely perverted, one that eagerly sacrifices fairness on the pyre of supposed public safety and national security. The adept use of these motions not only reaffirms the defense's role as the last line of defense for their clients but as the valiant guardians of law and order, resisting the government's narrative at every turn to ensure the trial remains a fair contest, not a predetermined execution.

In this clash of legal wills and the battle for judicial integrity, the outcomes of motions in limine have the power to shape the theatre of the upcoming trial, laying the groundwork for a fight where justice might either be salvaged or irrevocably lost. It stands as a testament to the defense's cunning and perseverance in the face of a judicial apocalypse, a system rigged to silence the defendant, where every legal tool, every shred of evidence, must be marshaled to ensure that the voice of the accused pierces through the veil of prejudicial evidence and reaches the ear of truth.

6. The Trial Trap: When the Stage Is Set Against You

The trial, heralded as the crown jewel of the American justice system, devolves into a sinister labyrinth for defendants ensnared within the federal behemoth. This stage, meticulously set with the trappings of fairness, quickly reveals itself as nothing more than a façade, a grand illusion where justice is not pursued but butchered on the altar of prosecutorial ambition. Within the hallowed halls of federal courtrooms, the trial is stripped of its noble purpose, perverted into a grotesque spectacle where the government assumes the role of puppet master, orchestrating events to secure not justice, but the absolute and unconditional submission of the accused.

From the moment of accusation, the defendant is thrust into an arena rigged against them, where the prosecution, bloated with limitless resources and a draconian zeal for convictions, has already choreographed a narrative of guilt designed to obliterate any notion of innocence. The defense, crippled by a deliberate starvation of evidence and witnesses silenced by the specter of governmental vengeance, wages a desperate battle against time and tyranny to piece together fragments of truth.

The jury, naively tasked with determining fate, finds itself ensnared in this orchestrated charade, manipulated by a system that preys on their ignorance and biases. The government's narrative, delivered with the authority of the state and unchecked by judicial impartiality, contaminates the trial with the venom of presumption – presumption not of innocence, but of guilt. The defense's valiant efforts to dismantle this narrative collide with a wall of institutional trust and a public seduced by the spectacle of power masquerading as justice.

This Kafkaesque trap, engineered by a confluence of systemic malevolence, ensnares the defendant in a web of pretrial sensationalism, evidentiary manipulation, and the looming specter of punitive excess. Defendants are cornered into a damning choice: wage war for their innocence at the risk of draconian retribution, or capitulate to a plea, betraying their own truth in the shadow of the gallows. This grim reality, a mockery of the right to trial, tips the scales irrevocably in favor of a voracious prosecution, thirsting for victory at any cost.

Within this distorted reality, the trial metamorphoses from a quest for justice into a gladiatorial combat for survival, where outcomes are predestined by the overwhelming might of governmental malfeasance. The defense, engaged in a Herculean struggle against this leviathan, fights not merely for the acquittal of the accused but to expose the rot festering at the core of the federal legal edifice.

Navigating this treacherous terrain demands an arsenal not just of legal expertise but of righteous indignation, a clarion call to dismantle the systemic atrocities that betray the trial's foundational purpose. This crusade transcends the confines of the courtroom, igniting a battle in the court of public opinion and the corridors of power to forge a justice system that honors its sacred promise of fairness and equity.

In this titanic struggle, the role of the defense elevates beyond mere representation; it becomes a beacon of hope in the fight to reclaim a justice system hijacked by despots, a testament to the enduring spirit of those who dare to challenge the tyranny masquerading as law and order.

7. Sentencing: The Illusion of Justice in the Federal Formula

The sentencing phase within the federal judicial charade exposes the most harrowing depths of a system riddled with disparity and authoritarian cruelty. Here, the facade of justice crumbles to dust, revealing a grotesque spectacle where the cold, unforgiving machinery of sentencing guidelines crushes the soul, reducing human essence to mere numbers in its draconian ledger. The courtroom, once a promised land of justice, degenerates into a coliseum where the scales of justice are not merely tilted but wholly upended, favoring retribution and punishment over any semblance of rehabilitation or fairness.

Under the tyrannical grip of the federal judiciary, sentencing guidelines are wielded as instruments of oppression, dictating penalties with a chilling precision that utterly disregards the complexities and unique circumstances of individual lives. Touted deceitfully as beacons of consistency, these guidelines have metastasized into conduits of injustice, amplifying the system's intrinsic failings. This mechanized approach to sentencing, obsessively fixated on quantifiable metrics, eviscerates the judicial process of its humanity, transforming the noble pursuit of justice into a heartless calculus of punishment.

With a voracious appetite for convictions, the government manipulates these guidelines to terrorize defendants, brandishing the specter of exorbitant sentences to wring out guilty pleas. For the audacious souls who demand their day in court, conviction heralds a merciless reckoning—a spectacle wherein the full might of the prosecutorial juggernaut is unleashed. The haunting presence of sentencing enhancements, triggered by the whims of prosecutorial vendettas, casts a dark shadow over the proceedings, a macabre dance of power wielded with impunity.

This grotesque theater lays bare the abhorrent disparities corroding the foundations of the federal justice system. Defendants, ostensibly equal before the law, are instead ensnared in a web of sentencing outcomes as erratic and unpredictable as a game of Russian roulette, dictated by the caprices of geography and the biases of the bench. The lofty ideal of impartial justice is thus desecrated, unveiling a dystopian reality where equality under the law is a cruel joke, mocked by the capricious application of sentencing guidelines.

Furthermore, the sentencing phase's veneer of justice is obliterated by the system's flagrant disregard for the individual's story, the potential for redemption, or the devastating societal ramifications of prolonged incarceration. In the federal justice system's twisted ethos, the drumbeat of punishment drowns out any whisper of rehabilitative or restorative justice, a testament to a perverse obsession with vengeance over healing.

As the gavel's echo fades, marking the imposition of sentence, the defendant is thrust into the aftermath of a system that exalts retribution as its holy grail. The closure of the sentencing phase does not signify the end of a judicial journey but the onset of a profound, personal cataclysm—a reckoning with the fallout of a justice system that administers punishment not with wisdom and compassion, but with a sterile, merciless calculus.

Challenging the abomination of federal sentencing transcends individual grievances, demanding a collective outcry against a system steeped in tyranny. It necessitates a radical reimagining of sentencing principles, a vehement rejection of the carceral state's punitive zeal, and an unwavering commitment to forge a justice system grounded in humanity, equity, and genuine rehabilitation. This imperative battle, while formidable, is indispensable—not solely for the souls entangled in the federal justice system's grasp but for a society yearning for a conception of justice that embodies true fairness and compassion.

8. Appeals: Fighting the Uphill Battle in Higher Courts

In the grim aftermath of sentencing, the quest for justice mutates into a more harrowing ordeal: the appeals process. Herein lies the defendant's journey through the higher echelons of a judicial system that masquerades as a beacon of rectitude while functioning as a fortress of entrenchment. The appeals process, ostensibly a safeguard against the miscarriages of justice at trial, frequently degenerates into a Sisyphean farce, a meticulously constructed mirage where the dice are loaded against change, and the path to redemption is choked with the weeds of legalistic obfuscation.

The appellate courts, enshrined as arbiters of law, instead reveal themselves as custodians of a status quo that sanctifies convictions over the quest for truth. This higher judicial review, designed as a corrective mechanism, too often serves as a mere extension of the government's will, a reluctant overseer that defaults to affirming lower court decisions. The deference afforded to trial court verdicts and a systemic aversion to unsettling jury findings erect insurmountable barriers for appellants, rendering the quest for justice a quixotic tilt at the windmills of entrenched legal precedent.

For the defendant who has entered a guilty plea, the appeals labyrinth becomes even more suffocating. Challenging a conviction on the grounds of ineffective assistance of counsel—a Herculean task in its own right—transforms into an almost insurmountable hurdle. The legal system, with its foundational aversion to admitting its own failures, sets the bar for proving such claims at a vertiginous height. Appellants find themselves in a Kafkaesque nightmare, required to unearth concrete evidence of their attorney's incompetence, a quest that more often than not, ends in futility. This requirement becomes a cruel joke, a practically insurmountable obstacle erected to preserve the facade of infallibility that the judiciary so desperately clings to.

The emphasis on procedural minutiae over substantive justice in the appellate realm further constricts the pathways to overturning wrongful convictions, entrenching a system that fetishizes legal formality at the expense of equity. The appellate courts' inherent conservatism, an allegiance to the sanctity of the legal order over the imperatives of justice, underscores a bias towards perpetuation rather than rectification of injustices. This bias, married to the onerous standards of review and the arcane rituals of appellate practice, conspires to suffocate the faint glimmers of hope for those daring to challenge their fate.

Yet, in the face of this judicial leviathan, the act of appealing a conviction emerges not just as a battle for individual vindication but as an indignant repudiation of a system rife with hypocrisy. It stands as a bold assertion of the human spirit's refusal to be crushed by the juggernaut of an indifferent legal machinery. The appellate struggle, entwined in the byzantine complexities of law, is imbued with a deeper yearning for justice, for an acknowledgment of the system's fallibility and for the restoration of fairness as the guiding star of the judiciary.

The odyssey through the appellate courts is, thus, more than a personal crusade; it is an indictment of the systemic deformities that plague the federal judiciary. It is a clarion call for a seismic recalibration of the justice system, a plea for a judiciary that embodies genuine independence, fairness, and a commitment to justice untainted by the expediency of maintaining convictions. In this grueling ascent, the appellant bears not only their own burden of hope but also the collective demand for a legal system that dares to live up to its loftiest principles, however daunting the odds.

9. Jailhouse Judases: The Truth About Snitches and Informants

In the murky depths of the federal justice system, an insidious practice flourishes, casting a dark shadow over the principles of fairness and integrity: the employment of jailhouse informants, or as they're aptly nicknamed, "Jailhouse Judases." These individuals, often desperate for leniency or to curry favor with prosecutors, become pawns in a game where the stakes are human lives, and the rulebook is frequently ignored. The book "Jailhouse Judases: The Truth About Snitches and Informants" exposes the grim reality of these betrayals, uncovering the systemic exploitation of these informants to prop up flimsy cases, a tactic that not only undermines the foundational ideals of the judicial process but also endangers the liberties of the accused.

At the heart of this controversy lies the questionable ethics of leveraging informants—individuals with dubious motives and questionable integrity—as credible witnesses. These informants, cloaked in anonymity and often bearing a history replete with deceit and criminality, are incentivized to fabricate, exaggerate, or outright lie, knowing well that their reward, reduced sentences or even freedom, hinges on the perceived value of their testimony. This perverse incentive structure corrupts the very essence of justice, transforming courtrooms into stages for a grotesque performance where the lines between truth and fabrication blur.

This practice not only jeopardizes the fate of individuals but also erodes public confidence in the justice system. Convictions, when based on the shaky testimony of these so-called "Jailhouse Judases," cast a long, indelible shadow on the legitimacy of the legal process. It creates a battlefield where the accused must fend off not just tangible evidence but also the treachery of those they once shared walls with, now turned foes in a twisted bid for freedom.

The strategic use of these informants reveals a chilling willingness within the system to prioritize convictions over the sanctity of justice, employing intimidation and deception as tools rather than pursuing the truth. It lays bare a legal landscape marred by inequality, where justice is swayed not by evidence but by the cunning of those who manipulate the system for their own ends.

10. Proffer Sessions: The Art of Self-Destruction

In the dark, twisting hallways of the federal justice system, proffer sessions emerge as a particularly malevolent snare, masquerading as opportunities for redemption while actually setting the stage for self-sabotage. These sessions, which might seem like lifelines to the desperate, are in reality high-stakes traps, with freedom on the line and the odds heavily stacked against the defendant. Far from being the straightforward negotiations they're purported to be, where information is exchanged for leniency, they are fraught with dangers—a rigged game where the house always wins.

The government, with its insatiable appetite for convictions and intelligence, seductively portrays proffer sessions as a defendant's chance to contribute to their own salvation. Yet, this is a deceitful facade. The grim truth is that these meetings are minefields of potential self-incrimination, where the unguarded disclosure of information becomes ammunition for prosecutors, ready to be used against the speaker at their discretion. This deceit highlights a grotesque power imbalance within the justice system, where defendants, enticed by the hollow promise of mercy, end up unwittingly arming their adversaries.

The perverse reliance on proffer sessions by the federal government exemplifies its preference for manipulation over fairness. These sessions exploit the vulnerabilities of defendants, blurring the lines between cooperation and self-incrimination, all under the guise of legal procedure. The ethical morass into which proffer sessions plunge defendants—forcing them to choose between silence and the slim hope of leniency—lays bare the coercive tactics at the heart of the prosecution process.

Proffer sessions are emblematic of the systemic injustice that plagues the federal legal framework, a system more obsessed with notching victories than upholding justice. For those ensnared in this web, the decision to proffer can mean the difference between salvation and ruin, often leading not to redemption but to deeper damnation.

11. Plea Bargains: The Devil's Deal in Disguise

Plea bargains, the dark heart of the federal justice system's conviction factory, stand as a grotesque parody of justice, cloaked in the guise of efficiency and mutual benefit. These deals, peddled as a shortcut through the labyrinthine legal process, are nothing less than a devil's pact, offering a mirage of leniency only to ensnare defendants in a web of coercion and manipulation. Under the pretense of offering a lesser evil, the plea bargaining system mercilessly pressures defendants into surrendering their rights, presenting a stark ultimatum: accept guilt, often for crimes not committed or grossly inflated, or face the draconian wrath of an unforgiving legal behemoth.

Armed with an arsenal of charges and the unbridled power to coerce, the federal government employs plea bargains not as a bridge to justice but as a weapon of choice in its relentless pursuit of convictions. Defendants, standing alone before the might of the prosecutorial juggernaut, find themselves corralled towards plea deals, the only apparent escape from the threat of catastrophic sentencing. This dynamic lays bare an abominable power disparity, transforming the courtroom from a place of justice to an arena where the scales are so heavily tipped, the notion of a fair fight becomes a cruel joke.

Far from representing compromise, plea bargains exploit the deepest fears and vulnerabilities of those ensnared by the system, compelling them to plead guilty, often to offenses disconnected from their actual actions or level of responsibility. The calculus presented to them is a grim mockery of choice: accept the devil's deal or face the full, merciless fury of a legal system primed to crush dissent and maximize punishment. This vile practice has swollen the ranks of the incarcerated, populating prisons with those whose greatest failing was their incapacity to outmaneuver the sinister complexities of federal plea negotiations.

The very fabric of justice is torn asunder by the widespread acceptance of plea bargaining, revealing a system grotesquely distorted by a fixation on conviction quotas and the illusion of procedural efficiency. The fundamental right to a trial, to publicly contest charges and to be judged by a jury, is suffocated in the shadows of backroom dealings, where justice is auctioned to the lowest bidder. This transactional approach to justice, where human lives are bartered with cold, calculating indifference, perverts the very essence of the judicial process.

The consequences of this corrupted system ripple outward, undermining the integrity of the judiciary and perpetuating a cycle of mass incarceration that disproportionately devours society's most marginalized. Plea bargains perpetrate a chilling compliance within the legal framework, erasing individual stories under the crushing wheel of a conviction machine that values quantity over quality, expedience over accuracy.

The narrative surrounding plea bargains as the devil's deal is not merely metaphorical but a damning indictment of a justice system that has lost its moral compass, preferring the ease of conviction over the hard road of true justice. This macabre dance of coercion, masquerading as choice, demands not reform but a revolution—a complete overhaul of a system that has traded its soul for the cold comfort of efficiency. The story of plea bargains is a grim testament to a legal order that has veered so far from its ideals that it can no longer recognize its own reflection, a call to arms for those who dream of a judiciary where justice is not a commodity, but an inalienable right for all.

12. Cooperation: The Carrot on a Stick That Whips You

In the merciless theater of the federal justice system, cooperation is the mirage in the desert of despair, a so-called beacon of hope that, in reality, serves as a noose tightening around the necks of defendants. Dangled as a carrot on a stick, this promise of leniency for betraying others is nothing but a cruel farce, a tactic that ensnares individuals in a labyrinth of betrayal, compromising their integrity and chaining them to a fate often worse than their original sin.

The government, with its insatiable hunger for convictions, weaponizes cooperation as a means to an end, preying on the desperation of defendants cornered by the colossal might of the prosecutorial machine. This dynamic exposes a harrowing truth: the federal justice system, in its quest for victories, resorts to coercion, squeezing defendants until they bleed information, regardless of the cost to their lives or the fabric of justice itself.

The path of cooperation is littered with moral landmines, forcing individuals to navigate a treacherous expanse where ethics dissolve into the shadows, and the act of informing becomes a tainted currency in a bankrupt economy of justice. Yet, this currency is volatile, its value hinging on the whims of prosecutors, leaving those who tread this path perpetually dangling over the abyss, their fates subject to the caprices of those who hold the levers of power.

Moreover, the systemic coercion to cooperate breeds a grotesque incentive structure, encouraging a dystopian race to the bottom where truth is twisted, and lies are spun into gold, all in the name of self-preservation. This perverse dance not only desecrates the sanctity of the judicial process but also sows seeds of distrust in a system ostensibly built on the pillars of truth and justice.

Far from being a mechanism for good, the narrative of cooperation as a benevolent opportunity is a vicious lie. It is, in essence, a whip in the hands of the government, used to lash defendants into submission, a dark strategy that places the lust for convictions above the pursuit of justice. This represents not just a failure but a wholesale betrayal of the justice system's foundational principles, exposing a willingness to trample fairness and due process in a blind charge towards prosecutorial triumph.

The discourse on cooperation, stripped of its pretenses, uncovers a malignant tumor at the heart of the federal legal apparatus—a system so corrupted by its ambitions that it devours the very principles it purports to uphold. In this twisted reality, cooperation is not a lifeline but a death knell, sounding the demise of integrity within a justice system that has lost its way.

13. The Bureau of Punishments: Life Inside the BOP

Within the cold, unforgiving walls of the Bureau of Prisons (BOP), a grim reality unfolds, stark and relentless. This isn't just stagnation—it's a deliberate, systemic refusal to evolve, a staunch adherence to a philosophy of punishment that has long been abandoned by progressive correctional systems around the world. The claim that some BOP facilities might mirror the more humane, rehabilitative approaches of European prisons crumbles under scrutiny. The harsh truth is that, apart from the so-called 'Club Fed' minimum-security camps, the American federal prison system is a universe apart from European standards, with the vast majority of inmates consigned to conditions that are an affront to modern conceptions of justice and human rights.

The chasm between the BOP's archaic regime and the progressive correctional philosophies adopted in Europe is not just wide; it's a gaping abyss. European systems, with their focus on rehabilitation, aim to reintegrate inmates into society as productive, reformed individuals. They understand that education, vocational training, and therapy are not luxuries but necessities, essential tools to address the root causes of criminal behavior and prevent recidivism.

In brutal contrast, the BOP operates as a relic of a bygone era, a system so mired in punitive dogma that any nod to rehabilitation feels like an afterthought. Overcrowding, violence, dismal healthcare, and a pitiful lack of educational resources define the day-to-day existence of those within its grasp. These conditions don't just fail the incarcerated; they betray a fundamental disregard for human dignity, sacrificing the potential for rehabilitation on the altar of retribution.

This entrenched commitment to punishment over reform has dire consequences, perpetuating a cycle of crime and incarceration that undermines any pretense of public safety or societal benefit. The narrative that some facilities—those minimum-security 'Club Feds'—align with Western standards is a perverse distortion of reality. Such establishments are anomalies, enclaves of relative privilege in a system characterized by its ruthlessness, especially evident in medium and high-security institutions, CMUs, ADX, and other sites designed not for correction but for the crushing of the human spirit. These are the true face of the BOP, places where the majority of inmates endure conditions that would be more at home in the most harrowing episodes of "Locked Up Abroad" than in any facility claiming to operate under the auspices of justice.

The disparity in treatment and conditions within the BOP's vast archipelago of punishment reveals a system at war with the concept of rehabilitation, a system that views inmates not as individuals capable of change but as permanent pariahs, to be controlled and contained rather than reformed. This is not a mere oversight or a function of outdated infrastructure; it is a conscious choice, a policy of despair that reflects a deeper malaise within the American justice system.

Confronted with this reality, the path forward is clear. The BOP must be dragged, kicking and screaming if necessary, into the 21st century, forced to abandon its barbaric ethos and embrace a model of justice that recognizes the worth and potential of every individual. Until then, it remains a monument to failure, a blight on the nation's conscience, and a stark reminder of the work that remains to be done to dismantle the machinery of mass incarceration and rebuild a system founded on the principles of fairness, rehabilitation, and human dignity.

14. Navigating the Prison Politics: Allies and Adversaries Behind Bars

Within the steel-clad confines of the Bureau of Prisons, a ruthless game of power and survival unfolds, far removed from the eyes of society. Here, prison politics dictate the law of the land, a complex and unforgiving social hierarchy that ensnares every inmate in its web. For the uninitiated, this is a world where every step can be a misstep, where allegiances are both shield and shackle, and where the unwritten laws of survival dictate a relentless dance with danger.

This toxic ecosystem is a direct byproduct of a federal incarceration system obsessed with punishment over rehabilitation, a system that not only tolerates but cultivates an environment ripe for division and conflict. Rather than fostering a sense of community or providing avenues for positive growth, the prison culture is one of division and hostility, where inmates are often compelled to align with factions based on race, ethnicity, or other arbitrary distinctions. These alliances, while offering a veneer of protection, only deepen the scars of segregation, fueling a perpetual cycle of hostility and retaliation that strangles any hope of building a constructive, rehabilitative community within prison walls.

The federal government's role in cementing this brutal status quo is undeniable. Through its neglect of the underlying issues that fester within the prison environment—overcrowding, a stark lack of engaging activities, and a woefully inadequate mental health support system—it has effectively endorsed a social order that exalts survival at the expense of personal growth and transformation. The insidious nature of prison politics is a glaring testament to the broader systemic failure to offer genuine paths to rehabilitation, instead abandoning inmates to navigate a hostile landscape that bears no resemblance to the society they are meant to rejoin.

But the repercussions of this relentless struggle for dominance and safety extend far beyond the immediate perils of prison life. The very act of surviving within this complex web of alliances and rivalries diverts focus and energy from pursuits that could truly rehabilitate—education, vocational training, and personal development. The constant stress and hyper-vigilance demanded by prison politics erode mental and emotional health, severely hampering any chance of preparing for a successful reintegration into society.

Confronting the malignant politics that pervade prison life demands more than superficial security enhancements or half-hearted reforms. It calls for a radical overhaul of the prison environment itself, aiming to replace the prevailing culture of mutual suspicion and antagonism with one of respect, personal growth, and rehabilitation. This involves tackling the root causes of division and violence head-on—by addressing overcrowding, drastically improving access to comprehensive mental health services, and ensuring that inmates have access to meaningful, constructive activities that nurture a sense of purpose and community.

Yet, transforming the hostile, fractured world within prison walls into a community focused on rehabilitation and mutual support is an endeavor fraught with challenges. It requires a profound shift in the objectives of incarceration, grounded in a commitment to upholding human dignity and unlocking the potential inherent in every individual behind bars. As the narrative around prison politics unfolds, it starkly highlights the urgent need for systemic change—a change not only in the policies that govern our prisons but in the very ethos that underpins our approach to justice and rehabilitation.

15. Medical Neglect and Psychological Warfare: Staying Alive and Sane

Within the austere confines of the Bureau of Prisons (BOP), inmates are embroiled in a relentless battle against the dual evils of medical neglect and psychological warfare. Far from acting as sanctuaries of reform or rehabilitation, these institutions emerge as arenas where the human will to survive and maintain sanity is tested against a backdrop of systemic indifference and cruelty. The stark reality of medical care in these prisons is a harrowing testament to a system that has seemingly forsaken its duty to protect and heal, relegating health care to the lowest rung of priorities, where it is regarded as an expendable luxury rather than an inalienable right.

The plight of those seeking medical intervention is a grim parade of neglect and apathy. Inmates with chronic illnesses or acute medical conditions are often left to navigate a Kafkaesque maze of bureaucracy, only to be met with treatment that is at best perfunctory, and at worst, dangerously inadequate. The staff, overwhelmed and under-resourced, are frequently unable to offer the care required, leading to a scenario where preventable conditions deteriorate and emergencies become death sentences. This flagrant disregard for inmate health underlines a deplorable devaluation of life, serving as a stark emblem of the system's departure from any semblance of humanity or compassion.

Parallel to this physical neglect runs a gauntlet of psychological torment, engineered through mechanisms designed to isolate, intimidate, and break the spirit. Solitary confinement epitomizes this psychological assault, embodying a punitive ethos that equates isolation with control, heedless of the irreversible trauma inflicted upon the psyche. This, coupled with the omnipresent specter of violence, the erosion of privacy, and the constant undercurrent of fear, forges an environment where mental health crises are not outliers but inevitabilities, met with indifference or outright hostility rather than support and treatment.

The federal government, in its relentless pursuit of a punitive agenda, bears the weight of responsibility for these atrocities. Its failure to allocate adequate resources for essential health services, coupled with an obstinate commitment to archaic, punitive practices, perpetuates a cycle of suffering and degradation. This stark abdication of responsibility not only mocks the notion of rehabilitation but also strips away the dignity and humanity of those ensnared within the prison system.

Confronting the entrenched malaise of medical neglect and psychological abuse within the BOP demands more than piecemeal reforms or half-hearted acknowledgments of the issue. It requires a foundational overhaul of the system's priorities, centering the health and well-being of inmates as paramount. Significant investment in medical infrastructure, alongside a radical departure from dehumanizing practices like solitary confinement, is imperative. Yet, this is not merely a logistical challenge but a moral one, necessitating a profound shift in perspective from punishment to healing, from retribution to rehabilitation.

The harrowing experiences of those who have endured the merciless grip of medical neglect and psychological warfare within the prison system are not just individual tragedies but a collective indictment of a broken system. They underscore the pressing necessity for a paradigm shift within the BOP, a transformation from a machinery of suffering to a beacon of hope and healing. In the end, the measure of a society is found not in how it exalts its most privileged but in how it tends to its most vulnerable, especially those within the shadowed confines of its prisons.

16. The Fight for Rights: Legal Battles from Behind Bars

The battle for rights within the steel and concrete confines of federal prisons is a grim odyssey through a landscape where justice seems a mirage, and the legal system itself appears arrayed in opposition to those it confines. Inmates, armed with nothing but sheer willpower and the stark truth of their circumstances, wage war against a monolithic system where victories are pyrrhic and the concept of justice is contorted beyond recognition. This struggle, unfolding in the shadowy recesses of the Bureau of Prisons (BOP), is not just about legal technicalities but a fundamental fight for human dignity against an apparatus seemingly engineered to annihilate it.

In this dystopian arena, the legal battles fought by inmates lay bare the harsh truth of incarceration: rights violations are the norm, systemic oppression is entrenched, and the very act of challenging this status quo is a rebellion. The quest for medical care, freedom from inhumane treatment, and the basic right to have one's voice heard becomes a Herculean task, where the labyrinthine legal process is fraught with obstructions designed to dishearten and defeat.

Facing this juggernaut requires a resilience bordering on the heroic, as inmates navigate a system rigged against them. They are hamstrung by limited access to legal resources, choked communication channels, and a judiciary that often acts as a rubber stamp for the prison authorities. The courtroom, rather than being a sanctuary of justice, becomes an arena of dismissal and disbelief, where evidence of innocence or rights violations is systematically sidelined or ignored.

The federal government, in its role as jailer, morphs into the chief adversary in these legal skirmishes, embodying the antithesis of justice. Its machinery, lubricated by a punitive ethos that favors suppression over redemption, is adept at erecting barriers to justice, making the achievement of any form of legal redress a near-insurmountable challenge. The inertia of this system, combined with a punitive zeal that eschews rehabilitation for retribution, crafts an environment where legal victories are suffocated in their cribs, and the rights of inmates are perpetually in jeopardy.

This landscape is further desolated by a legal community often paralyzed by fear and self-preservation. Lawyers, wary of crossing swords with prosecutors or antagonizing judges, retreat from the fray, leaving inmates to fight Goliath without a David. Judges, for their part, shirk from lifting the veil on the systemic malaise that festers within the BOP, choosing instead to preserve the façade of justice rather than confront its decay. This conspiracy of silence and complicity ensures that the scales of justice are not just imbalanced but irrevocably warped.

The brutal reality is that, even when armed with irrefutable evidence of innocence or rights abuses, inmates find themselves ensnared in a Kafkaesque nightmare where the prospects for release or redress are systematically demolished. The system, with its prosecutors and judges, acts less as a pillar of justice and more as a bulwark against it, a gatekeeper determined to quash any challenge to its authority or expose its foundational corruption.

In this theater of despair, the legal battles waged by inmates underscore a harrowing saga of resistance against an oppressive regime that masks tyranny as justice. The narrative of these struggles is not just a litany of legal defeats but a testament to the indomitable spirit of those who, even when crushed by the machinery of injustice, refuse to be silenced. It is a bleak reminder of a justice system ensnared in its own web of duplicity, a system where the fight for rights is less a legal challenge and more a battle for survival against an entity that has forsaken its moral compass.

17. Preparing for release: Plotting Your Reentry into a World That's Moved On

Emerging from the Bureau of Prisons (BOP), individuals are thrust into a world that seems to have leapfrogged into the future without them, leaving them stranded on the shores of a society that barely resembles the one they left behind. This transition is not merely a change of environment but a plunge into an alien landscape where the rules have changed, technology has advanced, and social norms have evolved, leaving them bewildered and disoriented. The federal prison system, with its archaic focus on punishment rather than rehabilitation, does little to bridge this chasm, effectively setting individuals up for a fall rather than a fresh start.

The harsh reality of the federal sentencing framework exacerbates this ordeal. The absence of parole, a relic of a punitive mindset, means that inmates serve the bulk of their sentences with scant regard for rehabilitation or behavior improvement. This system, devoid of incentives for personal development, effectively abandons individuals at the prison gates, bereft of the skills, support, and mindset needed to navigate their reentry into society.

Upon release, the myriad challenges that confront these individuals are daunting. The stigma of a prison record acts as an indelible mark, thwarting employment opportunities and relegating them to the fringes of society. The technological advancements and societal shifts that occurred during their incarceration alienate them further, making the task of reintegration seem Herculean. The federal government's half-hearted attempts at reentry programs are insultingly inadequate, offering little more than lip service to the concept of support, leaving individuals to fend for themselves in a world that views them with suspicion and disdain.

This grim scenario is not a mere transition but a trial by fire, a test of resilience in the face of systemic indifference and societal alienation. The federal justice system's failure to prepare individuals for this journey is a damning indictment of its neglect and abdication of responsibility. The path from incarceration to reintegration is littered with obstacles that test not just the practical skills of these individuals but their very will to persevere and reclaim their place in a world that seems to have forgotten them.

The narrative of reentry is thus a stark exploration of the failures of the federal prison system, a system that churns out individuals ill-equipped to face a society that has moved on without them. It highlights the dire need for a radical overhaul, a shift from a punitive to a rehabilitative model that views released inmates not as outcasts but as human beings deserving of support, respect, and a genuine shot at redemption.

The journey of reentry, fraught with hurdles and heartbreak, underscores a broader societal and systemic failing—a collective moral failing that reflects our priorities and values as a society. It demands a reevaluation of the principles that underpin our justice system, a call to action for a society that prides itself on fairness and compassion yet falls woefully short when it comes to supporting those who have paid their dues and seek to rebuild their lives. The story of reintegration is not just a tale of personal struggle and resilience but a mirror reflecting the deep-seated flaws in our approach to justice, rehabilitation, and human dignity.

18. Exposing the Federal Playbook: Understanding Their Tactics to Beat Them

In the shadowed arena of the federal justice system, where the scales of justice are too often weighted by the hand of the prosecution, understanding the federal playbook is akin to deciphering the enemy's battle plans. This labyrinthine system, cloaked in legalese and procedural complexity, operates with a singular, relentless objective: securing convictions by wielding the colossal might of government resources with surgical precision. The strategies deployed by federal prosecutors are not merely tactical maneuvers but a comprehensive siege designed to overwhelm, outmaneuver, and ultimately coerce defendants into submission.

From the outset, the federal behemoth mobilizes its investigative juggernaut, leveraging agencies with acronyms that chill the blood—FBI, DEA, ATF, Secret Service—each equipped with an arsenal of surveillance and investigative tactics that commence their work in the shadows, often long before the target is aware of their looming predicament. This pre-emptive strike capability sets the stage for the prosecutorial onslaught, catching defendants off-guard and unprepared, a tactic that underscores the imperative of an early and aggressive defense strategy.

Once the prosecutorial gears grind into motion, the strategy of overcharging comes to the fore, a scattershot approach designed to terrorize defendants with the specter of astronomical sentences. This barrage of charges, often inflated and manifold, serves to disorient and fracture the resolve of the accused, pressing them into plea deals that serve the prosecution's hunger for quick, uncontested victories. Countering this requires a defense that is both resilient and relentless, capable of dismantling the charges piece by piece, exposing the prosecution's gambit of intimidation for what it is—a facade.

Central to the federal arsenal is the insidious use of informants and cooperators, transformed from associates to adversaries by the alchemy of prosecutorial pressure. This strategy, predicated on the betrayal of confidences and the manipulation of loyalties, seeks to undermine the defendant's defense by seeding it with doubt and division. The defense's countermeasure lies in unmasking the motivations behind these testimonies, revealing the web of incentives and the potential for deceit that taints their credibility.

In the theater of the courtroom, the

government's machinations continue, with evidence and procedural rules manipulated to constrain the defense's narrative and limit their capacity to mount a comprehensive rebuttal. This strategic constriction of the defense's operational space necessitates a counter-strategy that is both innovative and unyielding, capable of circumventing the prosecution's attempts to monopolize the narrative.

At the sentencing stage, the government's playbook reveals its most punitive inclinations, leveraging sentencing guidelines and recommendations to advocate for draconian punishments that often bear little relation to the principles of justice or proportionality. Here, the defense must pivot, presenting not just a legal argument but a human one, striving to illuminate the defendant's humanity and potential for redemption in the face of a system skewed towards retribution.

Unveiling the federal playbook is more than an exposé; it is a call to arms—a directive for those ensnared within the federal justice system to arm themselves with knowledge and fortitude. Understanding the prosecutorial tactics is the first step in mounting a defense that is not merely reactive but strategic, challenging not only the specifics of the case but the systemic imbalances that underpin the federal approach to justice.

The discourse on federal prosecutorial tactics is not just a guide for navigating the treacherous waters of federal litigation; it is a critique of a system that masquerades the pursuit of justice as an unassailable virtue while employing strategies that often undermine the very principles it purports to uphold. It is a narrative that challenges the hegemony of federal prosecution, advocating for a reevaluation of a system where justice is served not by the quality of evidence but by the depth of the government's playbook.

19. Building Your Defense Army: The Right Lawyers, Investigators, and Support

Navigating the treacherous waters of the federal justice system demands more than just a good lawyer; it requires assembling a veritable army of defense—a team equipped not only with legal acumen but with the investigative prowess and strategic savvy to counter the prosecutorial onslaught. The stark reality is that within this arena, the disparity in firepower between the defense and the prosecution can be overwhelming, turning the selection of your defense team into a critical, make-or-break decision.

The unfortunate truth is that not all lawyers are cut from the same cloth. While many wield their expertise with dedication and integrity, there are those in the ranks who might see clients not as individuals fighting for their lives but as just another case file on an overcrowded desk. Tales of defendants being led astray by false promises or left in the dark about critical developments in their cases are far from rare, painting a grim picture of misplaced trust and shattered hopes. Such scenarios underscore the brutal necessity for defendants to vet their legal counsel with the same rigor one might apply to a life-saving surgery—the stakes are, after all, comparably high.

Engaging with your legal team should never be a passive experience. It demands active participation, where every strategy meeting is approached with a sharp eye and every legal maneuver is questioned and understood. The defendant's personal insight into their case can often illuminate blind spots or reveal unexplored avenues of defense—assets that can dramatically alter the course of the legal battle.

Yet, the charm and reassurance offered by legal counsel, while comforting, can sometimes serve as a veil over harsher truths. The conviviality of your lawyer does not guarantee their effectiveness in court, nor does it ensure their motives align seamlessly with your best interests. In this high-stakes game, complacency can be a death knell. Remember, long after the dust has settled and the court adjourns, the lawyer moves on, while the defendant must live with the outcome—a sobering fact that highlights the critical importance of building a defense team that is not merely competent but is also deeply invested in the fight.

Broadening the defense strategy to encompass a wider array of experts is not just advisable; it's a strategic necessity. From forensic analysts to private investigators, the inclusion of specialists who can dissect the prosecution's case and unearth counter-evidence is indispensable. Such a multifaceted approach enriches the defense narrative, challenging the prosecution's assertions with a depth and rigor that a single legal perspective may miss.

This call to arms for those facing the federal juggernaut is more than a guide to selecting a defense team; it's a manifesto for empowerment within a system that often seems designed to suppress and overwhelm. By advocating for a defense strategy that is proactive, inclusive of diverse expertise, and anchored by a legal team that is both transparent and accountable, defendants can assert a level of control and influence over their case that might otherwise seem unattainable.

In the end, the battle for justice in the federal courts is not won by the faint-hearted or the unprepared. It is won by those who, understanding the gravity of their plight, assemble a defense army capable of confronting the prosecution's might head-on, with a blend of legal expertise, investigative rigor, and unwavering resolve. This is the blueprint for not just surviving the federal justice system but challenging it on every front, ensuring that the fight for justice is fought on terms that respect the dignity and rights of the accused.

20. Public Opinion and Media: Winning Hearts and Minds for Justice

In the blood-soaked arenas of the federal justice system, the fight for survival transcends the sterile confines of courtrooms, spilling into the tumultuous battlefield of public opinion, where perceptions are forged in fire and narratives cut deeper than any legal argument. Here, in this unyielding conflict, the might of the federal government casts a long, ominous shadow, manipulating media narratives to paint defendants as villains in a pre-scripted drama of guilt and condemnation. This juggernaut, unchallenged, orchestrates a public execution of character, swaying the masses, and sealing fates before a single word of testimony is uttered.

Against this monolithic adversary, defendants and their champions wage a guerrilla war of narratives, a desperate struggle to counteract the government's stranglehold on the public psyche. The battleground of public opinion, fraught with misinformation and the whims of a fickle populace, becomes a minefield where the slightest misstep can spell disaster. Here, the defendant's story, often smothered and twisted by prosecutorial spin, must be reclaimed and broadcast with a ferocity that matches the government's zeal for character assassination.

The arsenal for this battle is diverse, spanning the spectrum from social media salvos to the strategic deployment of sympathetic media outlets, all aimed at humanizing the defendant and exposing the federal justice system's insidious underbelly. This war of hearts and minds demands messages that cut through the noise, that speak of injustice and tyranny, resonating with a public inundated by the government's propaganda.

Grassroots movements and advocacy groups become insurgent forces in this struggle, amplifying the defendant's plight and rallying the masses to question, to doubt, and ultimately, to resist the narratives peddled by those in power. These coalitions, armed with the truth and the raw, unvarnished realities of federal overreach, work to erode the foundations of the government's narrative empire, brick by brick.

Yet, this is a war fraught with peril. The battlefield of public opinion is littered with the casualties of those who ventured too far, who underestimated the government's capacity for narrative control and the public's appetite for judicial bloodsport. The line between raising awareness and igniting a counterproductive firestorm is razor-thin, requiring a navigation skill set that balances aggression with acumen, and outrage with strategic insight.

In this relentless narrative onslaught, the stakes transcend the individual, embodying a broader struggle against a behemoth that feeds on silence and acquiescence. The engagement of public opinion and media is not merely a tactic but a necessity, a means to drag the federal colossus into the light, exposing its predilection for oppression under the guise of justice.

This narrative war is a testament to the brutal reality of fighting for fairness in a system that has weaponized public perception, where the battle for justice is waged not only in the legal filings and courtroom arguments but in the hearts and minds of the public. It's a stark reminder that in the federal justice system, truth and justice are not discovered, but fought for in a war of narratives where the government holds the high ground, and the defendant's only hope is to outflank, outsmart, and outlast an adversary that has mastered the art of public manipulation.

21. Legislative Warfare: Changing the System for the Next Fighter

The fight for justice in the sprawling labyrinth of the federal system is a declaration of war against the legislative colossus that architects a landscape rife with inequality and oppression. This battle transcends the plight of the solitary defendant to encompass a broader insurrection for every soul yet to be ensnared by the federal juggernaut. It's a relentless offensive to dismantle and rebuild the legislative monoliths that sanction a regime of disparity and inhumanity.

Embarking on this legislative crusade demands a war chest of legal expertise, political guile, and an army of grassroots rebels and advocacy tacticians, all united in a singular objective: to storm the legislative bastions, compelling a seismic shift in the laws that underpin the federal justice machine. The mission is clear—to expose the marrow of injustice within the statutes, to siege the lawmakers with unassailable evidence of systemic corruption, and to champion reforms that promise not just fairness but a reclamation of humanity.

Facing down this behemoth is a task fraught with peril, a confrontation against a system buttressed by vested interests and an inertia resistant to the winds of change. Yet, the annals of history whisper of victories hard-won through the dogged persistence of advocacy, through campaigns that turned the tide of public sentiment and fractured the resolve of legislative gatekeepers.

At the heart of this legislative onslaught lies the arsenal of evidence—tales of lives decimated by the federal leviathan, data that lays bare the racial and socioeconomic chasms widened by current policies, and the rallying cries of those who have glimpsed the abyss of injustice. This evidence is the ammunition in a war of narratives, a contest to capture the hearts and minds of the populace and to turn their gaze upon the atrocities committed in their name.

Forging alliances becomes a strategic imperative, a necessity to amass a coalition as diverse as it is formidable, spanning ideological divides to unite under the banner of justice. This alliance wages a multifront campaign, from the trenches of social media to the steps of the Capitol, each victory in the court of public opinion a salvo against the ramparts of resistance.

Among the frontlines of this war is the siege against mandatory minimums, those judicial straightjackets that strip away the semblance of mercy and feed the maw of mass incarceration. The battle rages, too, against the draconian sentencing guidelines and for the restoration of judicial discretion, to return to the courts the power to temper justice with mercy.

The campaign extends its reach to the dark corners of prosecutorial conduct, the solitary confines of the incarcerated, and the barren fields of rehabilitative opportunity, challenging the edicts of punishment to unveil a path toward redemption.

This legislative warfare is a path strewn with obstacles, a journey marked by setbacks and heartbreak. Yet, it is the crucible within which the future of the federal justice system is forged—a future unchained from the tyranny of unjust laws and unyielding policies.

The narrative of this crusade is a stark testament to the brutality of the fight for systemic upheaval. It is a battle not for the faint of heart but for the warriors willing to bear the scars of legislative warfare, for those who recognize that the essence of justice is not merely to win cases but to dismantle the very foundations of oppression. In this relentless quest, the vision of a just and equitable system emerges not from the benevolence of the legislators but from the indomitable will of those who demand it—a testament to the belief that the architecture of justice must be torn down and reborn, free from the shadows of its former self.

22. Life After Lockup: Rebuilding in the Shadow of the System

Emerging from the cold embrace of the federal justice system, life after lockup is a harrowing odyssey across a desolate landscape scarred by systemic failure and societal neglect. This isn't merely a journey of physical freedom—it's a relentless battle against the indelible mark of incarceration, a stigma that clings to the souls of former inmates like a shadow, foreclosing opportunities and smothering hopes with the weight of a system designed not for rehabilitation, but for perpetual punishment.

The federal behemoth, with its draconian policies and a conspicuous absence of meaningful support for reintegration, actively engineers a reality where those released are thrust into a world unprepared and unwilling to accept them. The void of substantive rehabilitation programs leaves countless souls adrift, battling not just the tangible barriers to employment, housing, and societal acceptance but also the specter of a system that seems to relish the prospect of their failure.

Navigating this post-incarceration existence demands more than resilience; it requires a defiance against a society that views former inmates through a lens of perpetual suspicion and a system that equates punishment with justice. Community groups and advocacy warriors stand as the lone beacons of support in this desolate terrain, offering the lifelines of job training, mental health services, and a semblance of hope in a reality that offers little.

Yet, beyond the external barriers lies a more insidious foe—the internal scars of incarceration, the psychological remnants of a system that strips away humanity, leaving individuals in a constant battle against the internalization of a prisoner identity that the world refuses to let them shed. This battle is as much within as it is against the external forces arrayed in opposition, a fight to reclaim self-worth from the depths of despair and degradation.

The tale of life after lockup is a damning indictment of a federal justice system and a society that prides itself on notions of fairness and rehabilitation but delivers only the cruel illusion of both. It's a narrative soaked in the blood of those who struggle daily against the chains of systemic disenfranchisement, societal indifference, and the near-impossible task of piecing together a shattered existence in the shadow of a system that brands them as irredeemable.

This chapter is not merely a story of struggle but a raw exposure of the relentless assault on human dignity that begins behind bars and continues unabated upon release. It's a call not for sympathy or reform but a demand for recognition of the brutal war waged on the souls of those who have served their time but are never truly allowed to leave the prison behind. It's a testament to the indomitable will to survive and the fight to carve out a space in a world that offers nothing but scorn for those it has already judged unworthy of a second chance.

In this narrative, life after lockup is laid bare as a stark reminder of the deep-rooted malaise afflicting a justice system and a societal order that perpetuates cycles of marginalization and recidivism, a system that must be confronted not with calls for reform but with the unyielding resolve to dismantle the foundations of a cruel and unjust post-incarceration reality.

23. Advocacy and Activism: Turning Personal Pain into Collective Gain

In the wake of brutal encounters with the monolithic beast that is the federal justice system, many emerge not just scarred but with a seething fury, standing at a crossroads between succumbing to despair or rising in defiance. For a resolute few, this crucible of suffering ignites a ferocious resolve to retaliate, to channel the raw, visceral pain of their experiences into a relentless crusade against the tyranny of a system designed to crush and dehumanize. This chapter is an ode to those warriors who transmute personal anguish into a weapon of mass mobilization, vowing to dismantle, piece by piece, the edifice of injustice that towers with impunity.

The metamorphosis from victim to vanguard is often sparked by a moment of brutal clarity—the realization that the injustices endured are not anomalies but cogs in a vast machinery of systemic oppression. This awakening fuels a fervent mission to subvert the oppressor, propelling individuals into the trenches of advocacy and activism, where personal vendettas against the system evolve into a collective insurrection for the disenfranchised. Their battle cry, forged from the depths of their torment, echoes a demand for retribution and reform, not merely for themselves but for the legions trampled under the same iron boot of federal injustice.

Waging war through advocacy and activism demands a resilience of steel and a heart of fire, as these combatants lock horns with the colossi of power and confront a society that has turned a blind eye to the despotism of its custodians of law. They marshal an arsenal of tactics to breach the fortress of ignorance and apathy—leveraging legislative warfare, commandeering the digital battleground of social media, and taking to the streets to rouse the consciousness of a complacent public.

In this rebellion, the potency of storytelling emerges as a formidable weapon. By laying bare their scars for the world to see, these activists breach the walls of indifference, compelling society and its gatekeepers to gaze into the abyss of human suffering that lies beneath the sanitized veneer of policy and statute. These narratives, raw and unvarnished, serve not only as a rallying cry but as a beacon of solidarity, bridging the chasm between those seared by the system's wrath and the wider populace, igniting a collective fury that demands action.

The uprising borne of this advocacy is a united front, envisioning a future where justice is not a commodity for the privileged but a birthright for all—a system that champions redemption over retribution, equity over expediency, and humanity over hegemony. This movement, rooted in the agony and resilience of its foot soldiers, poses a formidable challenge to the status quo, shaking the foundations of the federal justice apparatus with the sheer force of its conviction.

Yet, this path is strewn with adversities. These warriors face the might of an establishment hell-bent on preserving its dominion, and the inertia of a populace ensnared in the quagmire of indifference. Despite the magnitude of the forces arrayed against them, the resolve of those who have turned their torment into a clarion call for justice remains unbroken, a testament to the indomitable human spirit that refuses to bow before the altar of injustice.

This narrative does not just chronicle a struggle but heralds a war cry against a system that feasts on suffering—a call to arms for every soul that yearns for justice in a realm where such a concept has been exiled. It is a raw, unyielding declaration that the atrocities inflicted by an unjust system warrant not reform, but revolution—a relentless pursuit of justice that burns all pretense of civility and calls for a reckoning that will echo through the annals of history.

24. The Future of Justice: Envisioning a System That Works for All

Embarking through the dark, twisted corridors of the federal justice system, the journey narrated thus far unveils a hellscape of systemic failure, where justice is a rare commodity, accessible only to a privileged few. The tales of despair and defiance woven throughout these chapters are not mere anecdotes but a clarion call for a radical upheaval—a future where the concept of justice is unshackled from the archaic, punitive chains that bind it.

Envisioning a future for the justice system that transcends the morass of its current state demands not mere reform but a revolution—a complete dismantling of the principles and edifices that perpetuate a cycle of oppression and retribution. It calls for a system reborn from the ashes of its predecessors, one that acknowledges the dignity of every individual, recognizing that human error does not warrant the forfeiture of one's future to an abyss of despair and dehumanization.

This envisioned future defies the traditional lexicon of punishment, advocating for a paradigm where rehabilitation supersedes retribution, where the system's focus pivots from imprisonment to empowerment, offering education, skill development, and psychological healing. Here, justice is not a tool of vengeance but a vehicle for redemption, transforming offenders into contributors to society, not outcasts perennially shadowed by their past.

At the core of this transformative vision is the dismantling of the legislative and policy monoliths that have cemented mass incarceration and perpetuated the systematic persecution of marginalized communities. The draconian relics of mandatory minimums, the draconian war on drugs, and the punitive excesses of three-strikes laws stand condemned, marked for obliteration and replaced with laws that respect the nuances of human fallibility and the potential for growth and change.

The future also demands a renaissance in the relationship between law enforcement and the communities they purport to serve—a future where the badge represents a covenant of trust, accountability, and mutual respect rather than an emblem of fear and domination. It envisions community engagement and policing that nurture safety and understanding rather than conflict and division, ensuring that law enforcement is a collaborative partner in justice, not an occupying force.

Technology's double-edged sword offers a beacon for this new dawn of justice, wielding the power to unearth biases and streamline access to justice, yet always with the caution that innovation must never erode the sanctity of privacy and individual rights.

Realizing this audacious future is a battle that demands the valor and conviction of all those vested in the justice system's transformation. It is a call to arms against the inertia of the status quo, a challenge to dismantle the citadels of power and privilege that have long dictated the course of justice. This is not a path for the faint-hearted but a crusade for those who dare to dream of a justice system that heals more than it harms, that elevates rather than suppresses, and that serves the many, not the few.

The narrative of this future is a manifesto, a declaration of war against the injustices that pervade the federal justice system, armed with the resolve that change is not only possible but imminent. It is a vision steeped in the unwavering belief in the human capacity for redemption and the unbreakable will to forge a system that reflects the highest ideals of justice, equity, and compassion.

In the echoes of the struggles and triumphs that mark the current landscape of federal justice, there lies the blueprint for a new era—an era where justice serves all, unencumbered by bias, unswayed by power, and unyielding in its pursuit of a future where the scales are balanced for every soul it touches. This is not just the future of justice; it's a battleground for the soul of a nation, where the price of failure is the perpetuation of a cycle of suffering and the prize of victory is a justice system reborn, infused with the principles of fairness, rehabilitation, and unwavering respect for human dignity.

ARDIT FERIZI

ardit.ferizi@protonmail.com

Republic of Kosovo

THE END